Annamarie,
   I hope you enjoy this. It was written by a very good fri Craner, and the pictures were drawn by her daughter Jocelyn.
   I love you ♡
   Grandma

PEACOCK IN THE PINE TREE

Written by Sandra Cramer
Illustrated by Jocelyn Cramer

A Grackle Book

Grackle
An imprint of Grackle Publishing, LLC
gracklepublishing.com

Copyright © 2018 Sandra Cramer
Illustration Copyright © 2018 Jocelyn Cramer
All rights reserved.
ISBN: 978-0-9982069-7-4

This is a work of fiction. Names, characters, places, and incidents either are the products of the author's imagination or are used fictitiously. Any resemblance to actual persons, living or dead, businesses, companies, events, or locales is entirely coincidental.

FOR EVERY GRAMMY'S COOKIE, ESPECIALLY MINE…

ANTHONY, COLE, SETH AND CHLOE

I WOKE UP ONE MORNING

AND WHAT DID I SEE?

A BIG OLD PEACOCK

IN MY BACKYARD PINE TREE.

WE SMILED EAR TO EAR

AS WE STARED EYE TO EYE,

THEN HE JUMPED FROM THAT TREE

WITH A LEAP

TOWARD THE SKY!

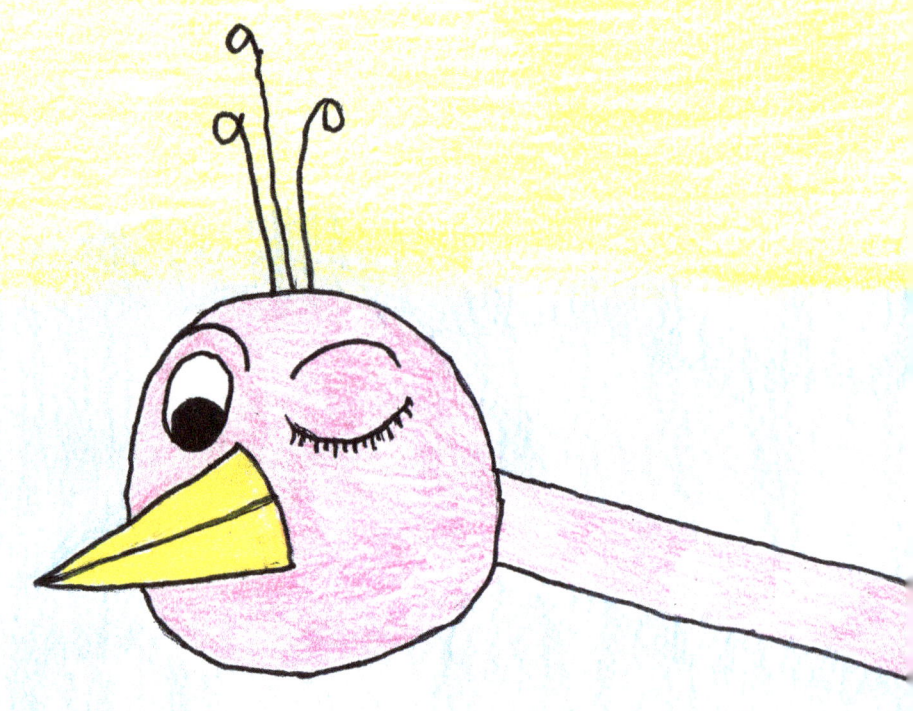

A NUDGE, THEN A TWIST

TURNED HIS TAIL TO FACE ME.

HIS TAIL FANNED OUT WIDE,

**RAINBOW COLORS
 SWIRLED AROUND!**

SPARKLY AND SHINY...

A TREASURE I'D FOUND!

ALL MY NEIGHBORS GATHERED TO SEE THIS BEAUTIFUL SIGHT.

WHERE DID HE COME FROM?

WILL HE STAY HERE ALL NIGHT?

HE FLUFFED SOME RUFFLED FEATHERS USING HIS FOOT FOR A COMB.

WE HEARD HIS OWNER, JOE, GIVE A WHISTLE!

IT WAS TIME TO GO HOME.

WE ALL CLAPPED AND CHEERED AS HE WALKED OUT OF SIGHT,

COOL!

YAY!

AWESOME!

WOW!

GREAT!

THEN UNDER THE MOONLIGHT BID EACH OTHER, "GOODNIGHT!"

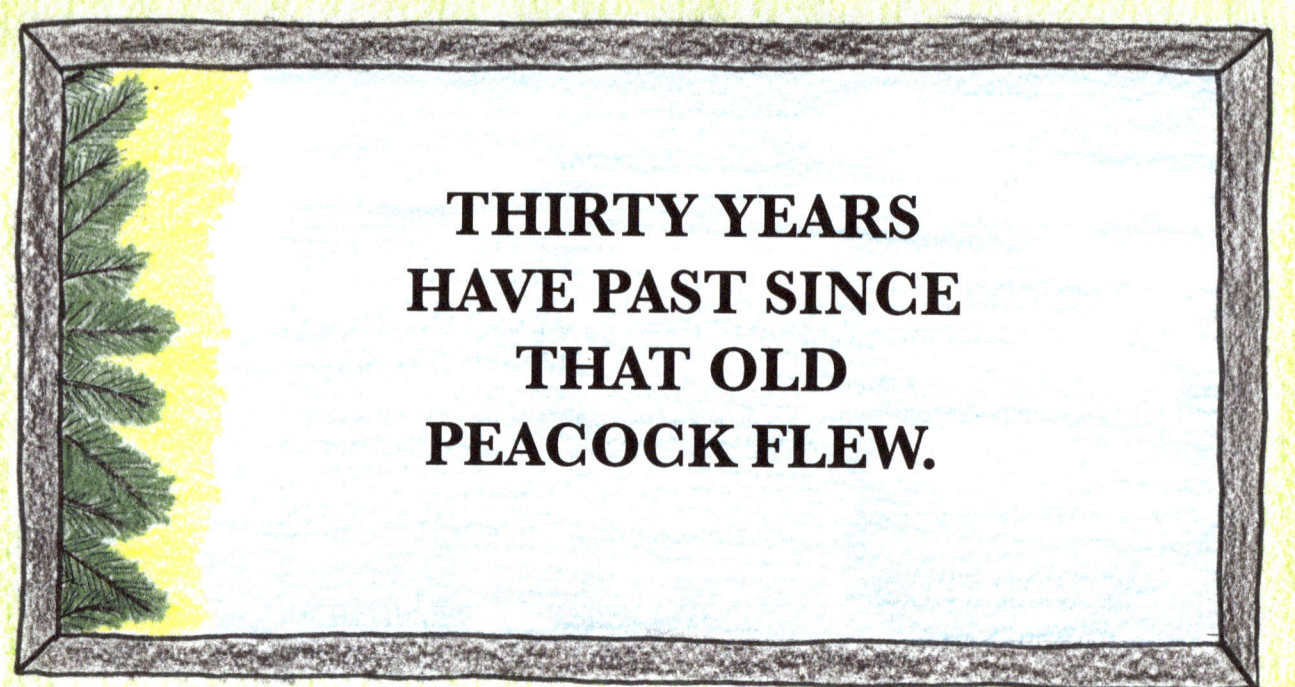

THIRTY YEARS
HAVE PAST SINCE
THAT OLD
PEACOCK FLEW.

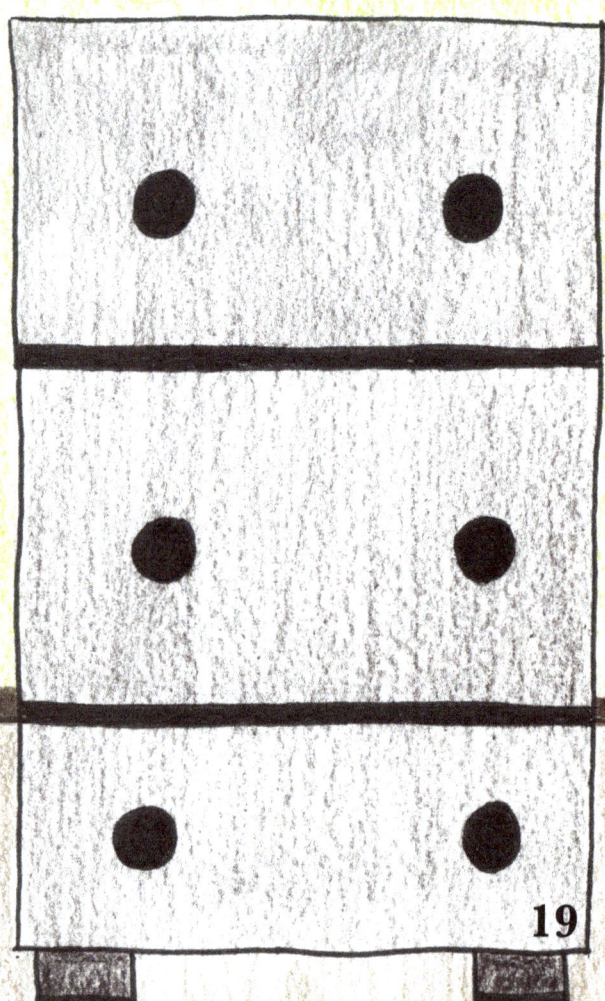

I STILL TELL THIS STORY,
 SHOW THE FEATHERS HE DROPPED,
 AND BELIEVE
  IN VERY SPECIAL DAYS...

DON'T YOU?

THE END

A Grackle Book

CPSIA information can be obtained
at www.ICGtesting.com
Printed in the USA
BVHW02*1628260218
509108BV00003B/3/P